NATURAL DISASTERS

WILDFIRE!

BY MARION DANE BAUER

ILLUSTRATED BY JOHN WALLACE

Ready-to-Read

Simon Spotlight
New York Amsterdam/Antwerp London
Toronto Sydney/Melbourne New Delhi

For my grandchildren
—M. D. B.

To Abi
—J. W.

SIMON SPOTLIGHT
An imprint of Simon & Schuster Children's Publishing Division
1230 Avenue of the Americas, New York, New York 10020

This Simon Spotlight edition May 2026

Manufactured in the United States of America 0326 LAK
10 9 8 7 6 5 4 3 2 1
CIP data for this book is available from the Library of Congress.
ISBN 9798347102860 (hc)
ISBN 9798347102853 (pbk)
ISBN 9798347102877 (ebook)

GLOSSARY

arson (say: AR-sin): the willful act of burning property.

back-burning fires: setting controlled fires to remove fuel from the path of a wildfire.

climate: the average environmental condition of a place over a period of years.

drought (say: DROWT): a prolonged period of dryness.

firebreaks: areas of cleared land that slow down or stop the spread of fire.

underbrush: shrubs, bushes, or small trees growing under the large trees in woods or forests.

Note to readers: Some of these words may have more than one definition. The definitions above match how these words are used in this book.

Fire has been our friend
for a very long time.
From our early days,
fire cooked our food.

Fire lit up the dark.

Fire kept us warm.

Fire even moved us faster than ever before.

But when fire burns
out of control,
it is not our friend.

Then it is called wildfire.

Some wildfires are
caused by lightning.
Or made worse by
the heat of the sun.

A very few are caused
by erupting volcanoes
or by large meteorite strikes.

But most wildfires are caused by careless people.

Untended campfires.

Fallen power lines.

Fireworks.

Cigarettes.

Arson.

Wildfires are made worse
by hot weather
and by **drought**.

That means our changing **climate** brings more wildfires.

Specially trained firefighters fight wildfires with water or chemicals.

They even
fight fires from
helicopters
or airplanes.

They create **firebreaks** so that fire runs out of fuel. They set **back-burning fires** to use up fuel too.

Once, we tried to stamp out every forest fire as soon as it started.

But that led to a buildup of decaying grass, shrubs, and leaves on forest floors.

This fuel created bigger wildfires.

Now we let small fires burn to keep the forest floor clear. We even set fires to burn away fuel.

We thin **underbrush** too.
A fire cannot start
without a source
or grow without fuel.

Wildfires hurt many creatures. They burn down houses as well.

They also leave behind floods and eroding soils, polluted water and air.

Even so, our Earth knows how to heal.

When the fire dies down,
ashes nourish the soil.

And life returns.

INTERESTING FACTS

- There are three types of wildfires. Ground fires burn underground, eating up roots and rotting plants. Surface fires burn along the top of the ground. Crown fires leap from treetop to treetop. All three types can happen in the same fire.

- Fire needs three things to burn: heat, fuel, and oxygen. This combination is called the fire triangle.

- Lightning strikes somewhere on Earth more than eight million times a day. Under the right conditions, a wildfire can start from a lightning strike.

- Wildfires occur most often in places that are hot and dry.

- Some forms of life make use of fire. Fire beetles lay their eggs in smoldering trees. Several evergreen trees need fierce heat to release their seeds.

- Native people used to set controlled burns to keep forests healthy. Modern fire management science is finally learning from native fire practices.

- The temperature of a wildfire can be higher than 2,000 degrees Fahrenheit.

- Big wildfires can make their own weather. They can create clouds with lightning, and they can bring about rain and winds as strong as a hurricane.

- Wildfires release carbon dioxide and other greenhouse gases into the air, making global warming worse. More global warming brings more wildfires.

To learn more about wildfires and fire safety, ask a trusted adult to reach out to your local fire department for more information.